AUSTRALIAN
BUSH VERSE

A TALE OF TERMITES II
Oil on hardboard 45 cm × 35 cm 1976

AUSTRALIAN
BUSH VERSE

*Selected from
The Bronze Swagman
Book of Bush Verse*

Illustrated by Maynard Waters

URE SMITH

Sydney·Auckland·London·New York

Published by Ure Smith, Sydney
a division of Paul Hamlyn Pty Limited
176 South Creek Road, Dee Why West, NSW, Australia 2099
First Published 1976
2nd Impression 1979
Paintings © Maynard Waters 1976
Poems (this selection) © Ure Smith 1976
Produced in Australia by the Publisher
Designed by Snape and Gallaher Graphics, Sydney
Typeset by Savage and Co. Pty Ltd, Brisbane, Qld.
Printed in Singapore by Kyodo Shing-Loong Printing Industries Pte Limited
National Library of Australia Card Number and
ISBN 0 7254 0344 6

Preface

In our increasingly urban society where practically everything can be bought in a department store or supermarket, where there's an expert professional to advise on or perform any service that anyone might require, it is heartwarming to know that "the Australian way of life" as most of us idealize it — though relatively few actually live it — is flourishing still. This book, through both the verse and the paintings, provides delightful evidence of the fact.

The town and district of Winton in outback Queensland have a long-established link with bush verse, for it was at Dagworth Station near Winton that that most famous of all Australian poets, "Banjo" Paterson wrote "Waltzing Matilda".

In 1970 the newly-established Winton Tourist Promotion Association, in an effort to raise funds, published *Matilda-Matilda: a Whole Swagful of Local Verse.* This small booklet, produced on a Fordigraph machine under extremely difficult conditions, proved so popular that orders were received from all over the world, even Russia, and a second printing was required.

And so the idea of the annual Bronze Swagman Award for Bush Verse was born. In five years the number of entries for the Award has soared from 172 in 1972 to 760 in 1976, and entries have been received from all over Australia, from New Zealand, England, Germany and the United States. The best entries each year are published in *The Bronze Swagman Book of Bush Verse,* and the first prize winner receives a bronze statuette of the Waltzing Matilda Swaggie by Australian sculptress Daphne Mayo and a Winton opal.

The poems are highly original, warm, sad, witty, lyrical, nostalgic, sometimes bawdy or hilariously funny — in short, they cover the full range of traditional Australian bush verse.

For this book the publishers made a selection of verse from each of the booklets, and were delighted when Maynard Waters agreed to illustrate them with a series of oil paintings. Of course we already knew the quality of his work, and we knew that his style, his sense of humour, his nostalgic view of the romantic outback, would admirably suit both the subject matter and the style of the verse. But we were overwhelmed and delighted with the finished paintings. We feel that he has captured the quintessential spirit, not only of the verse, but of a whole way of life with which most Australians identify strongly.

Our warm thanks to the Winton Tourist Promotion Association for their willing co-operation and assistance, to the individual poets whose work is included, and to the many whose verse, due to lack of space, is not, for the task of selection was not an easy one. Our thanks, too, to Maynard Waters, for the sympathetic and lively understanding he has brought to his interpretations of the verse.

THE ONE MAN TOWN
Oil on hardboard 45 cm × 35 cm 1976

Contents

Timber Town

Row of shacks along the railway, timber houses on the rise;
Humming saws and creaking benches, dusty roads and dusty skies;
Blackbutt forests on the mountain, timber jinkers winding down;
Sawdust pile and stack of sleepers: just another timber town.

Barefoot children in the roadway, old men dozing in the sun,
Dogs and goats and scraggy horses, fences falling one by one.
Church and hall and store and butcher, old-time pub of tough renown —
Travellers pass it in a hurry, just another timber town.

In the churchyard, leaning headstones cover up the storied past;
Men who tamed the rugged country resting from their toil at last.
Men who knew the lust of living, bite of hope and sting of tears,
Singing, laughing, sweating, swearing, loving, living down the years.

Forty miles along the highway northern city's neons shine
Calling to the dreams of youth, as long ago they called to mine.
I've searched the world and found the answer, coming time to settle down,
Build a home and raise a family, back in my own timber town.

ERIC WATSON

TIMBER TOWN
Oil on hardboard 35 cm × 45 cm 1976

A Tale of Termites

STRANGER please pause by this old bungalow
For it hides a grim battle that ebbs to and fro,
A primitive struggle devoid of romance,
'Twixt the Camooweal drunks and the giant white ants.
No quarter is given, no mercy displayed,
In this fight to the death with the termite brigade,
But if their rampaging is not soon reduced,
You can all say goodbye to the old ringer's roost.

There are termites to left and termites to right,
And their molars are grinding by day and by night;
They raid and they ravage and plunder unchecked,
And they're larger, much larger, than one would expect.
By wall plate and rafter they stealthily creep,
And God help our hides if they catch us asleep.
And if we can't turn their attack mighty soon,
We'll be under the stars by the change of the moon.

There are white ants below and white ants above,
In the floorboards and battens and rafters they love,
They deploy to the left and attack from the right,
And their molars are grinding by day and by night.
They break up our parties and ruin our rest,
And they are in a nutshell a damnable pest;
And if we can't deal them a kick in the slats,
I fear it's the end of these bachelor flats.

We've tried every method to stop their advance,
We've fought them with poison and baton and lance,
But it does little good, for in thousands they breed,
And they sharpen their fangs as they look for a feed.
An expert once called in to give us a quote,
But as soon as he entered they sprang at his throat.
He fought himself free with the leg from a bed,
And "One flick and I'm going," he screamed as he fled.

A TALE OF TERMITES I
Oil on hardboard 35 cm × 45 cm 1976

They've ravaged our larder, our furniture too,
And one night they punctured a carton of brew,
Then the word got around to the whole of their tribe,
And they bunged on an orgy I couldn't describe.
They've cleaned up our woodheap, our outhouse as well,
The "man who comes round" said he'd see us in Hell;
They've eaten our moleskins and eaten our Bex —
Two novels by Thwaites and a pamphlet on sex,
And if very soon we don't stop their advance,
Then I'll transfer the deeds to the flamin' white ants.

B. F. SIMPSON

A TALE OF TERMITES II
Oil on hardboard 45 cm × 35 cm 1976

An Old Mate

I MET him in a country pub one sultry summer's day;
I'd come to town to have a binge, I'd just received my pay,
The bar was quite deserted, just this other bloke and me,
And I reckoned by the way he looked he needed company.

I introduced myself to him and bought a round of beer,
And said, "Just tell me where to go if you don't want me here."
He looked at me and gave a grin and said, "You're welcome, mate."
The story that he told to me I'd like here to relate.

"I had a friend," he said to me, "the greatest mate I knew,
And I could always count on him if I was in a blue,
When work was short and money scarce old Blue was right by me,
And in good times when I'd a quid we'd both go on a spree.

"We were running scrubber cattle out the Thargomindah way,
Wild cows and cleanskin mickeys were the order of the day,
When scrub bulls bailed and stirred for fight, old Blue was there with me,
He'd fight them till their spirits broke — the gamest dog you'd see.

"We bailed a crossbreed late one day, a big bull, strong and straight,
Wide upswept horns and matted tail and mad eyes filled with hate;
I knew that Blue was tired and hot, we'd had a long dry day,
I also knew that bull was bad, he'd make me earn my pay.

"I yelled to Blue to stay behind and drove my stock horse past.
I swear to God I've never seen a bull that turned so fast;
I tried to turn my pony round, I know he gave his best,
The bull came charging straight and fast and gored him in the chest.

"My horse fell with a scream of pain and smashed me to the ground.
I felt my right leg snap in two, and blood was all around,
I saw that wild bull turn around — I knew this was the end —
When Blue dashed out to help his mate: he'd come to save a friend.

"He grabbed that bull low on the nose and tried to pull him down;
The scrubber roared with pain and fear and smashed him to the ground,
But Blue he hung on to that nose, he gave his life for me
As that wild bull wheeled quickly round and crushed him on a tree.

"Then like a flash the bull was gone, and Blue lay stiff and still:
I knew that he had gone to rest, he'd climbed his last long hill.
The others found me where I'd crawled to safety by a log;
They carried that old mate back home — my faithful cattle dog."

PAUL HARROWER

AN OLD MATE
Oil on hardboard 35 cm × 45 cm 1976

The Mail Truck — Winton

Now I rode on one of the mail runs
    And I'll tell of one of the days,
So take off your hat to the mailmen
    As you speed on your bitumen ways.

We start off due south in the darkness
    With the truck piled high with gear,
While the squat-roofed old town is still sleeping
    And the stars in the sky shining clear.

Then we jerk up the sandstone escarpment,
    See the grey-shadowed plains lie below;
Soon the feathery bush cuts a black frieze
    Against sunrising's apricot glow.

The turning mill heralds each station
    As we swing to a narrower road,
Dump the mail bag, some feed and some tucker
    And bore casing which lightens the load.

Some stations sank bores in the good times,
    There's citrus and tennis discussed.
Some stations are raw but undaunted,
    There's sun and hot tin and red dust.

We inch in low gear round the washouts,
    Then find that the waterbag's burst;
A swollen pig breaks the creek's surface
    Just after we've slaked a long thirst.

One home creek is full of brown water
    From a storm at the end of July,
The galahs all exclaim in the branches,
    A startled grey horse splashes by.

We clatter and sway into Mayneside
    Where the old homestead's creepers entwine
And cover the ant-eaten timbers
    Which are scarred by the ravage of time.

The motes of dust tickle our nostrils
    Off-loading the last wheaten hay:
"It's come far too late now to save us."
    Four o'clock and the end of the way.

THE MAIL TRUCK – WINTON I
Oil on hardboard 45 cm × 35 cm 1976

Old spinifex clumps sharp erupting
   From anthracite blue pebbly sands,
And Don smears his sun-dazzled vision
   With the back of a sweat-begrimed hand.

Old opal shafts pock-mark the country
   Where fevered men hacked out the rock;
Uneatable — drinkable gem stones —
   The pitiful holes seem to mock.

Back to the road and the township
   Where street lights gleam white on the plain
And in between, all the vast country
   Keeps watch through earth's ages for rain.

M. PERRIN

THE MAIL TRUCK – WINTON II
Oil on hardboard 35 cm × 45 cm 1976

The Times When the Seasons are Good

ENOUGH has been written of flood times
Of drought we've heard time and again,
So let me now tell of the good times:
Good seasons with plenty of rain.

Remember the times when our cattle
Brought premium prices at sales?
The bids that came in with a rattle
From the buyers all perched on the rails?

The horses that won in a canter
When the local race meetings were run?
The drinking, the yarns and the banter
Round the bar when the meeting was done?

The flowers and the birds all so pretty
On the land when the seasons are good,
Are things that the folk in the city
Never see, but I wish that they could.

When the seasons are good and the grasses
Grow green, thick and high on the hill,
The time simply flies as it passes
If we pause and remember them still.

W. J. McGUIGAN

THE TIMES WHEN THE SEASONS ARE GOOD
Oil on hardboard 35 cm × 45 cm 1976

Boolem

HAVE you been told of Boolem in the Never-Never Land?
The farmers harvest gibbers and they dam the drifting sand;
The sun dries the mirages as they float across the plain;
But no one talks of drought because they've never heard of rain.

The stock they raise are hardy goats with fleece as fine as silk,
And from the herd they get supplies of dehydrated milk.
They haven't any trees there, not even fallen logs,
For years ago the trees pulled out and went to look for dogs.

A stranger came to Boolem with his throat all parched and raw;
They offered him a drink and said, "It's water from the bore."
"Good grief!" exclaimed the startled man. His eyes grew round and big:
"I hope you can assure me that it is a healthy pig!"

The fishermen of Boolem are the best in all the land;
The fish they catch are gropers and they grope for them in sand.
A youngster caught a tiddler once and kept it in a dish;
His mother poured some water in and drowned the muddy fish!

If tourists visit Boolem town, they always want to stay,
Pretending it's the climate spilling sunlight every day;
But when they come to Boolem and they want to stay a year,
The reason is, the water's off and all they drink is beer.

ALF WOOD

BOOLEM
Oil on hardboard 35 cm × 45 cm 1976

The New Breed Salesman

WE lived an ordered family life
   With clothes and habits sane,
Detesting fancy modern things
   And grim pollution's stain.

And strangers almost to a man
   Were welcome at our place,
No matter where they travelled from,
   Their colour or their race.

He slowly walked with shoulders dropped,
   Full beard and drooping mo.
And looking like a lizard lost,
   But cunning as a crow.

We watched him walk across the yard,
   His dry long lanky locks,
And pointed toes — a purple shade —
   Plus psychedelic socks.

And soft mauve shirt and pants to match,
   Both branded "Never crease",
A long broad tie with bulging knot
   The colour — pale cerise.

Not hard to see the old man watched
   With eagle-eyed disdain,
All out of place 'mid these surrounds,
   A new exotic strain.

Indulging not in platitudes
   Came quickly to the point
And dropped his case upon the ground:
   "The owner of this joint?

"I represent a Brisbane firm,
   The House of 'With-it Gear',
Men's toiletries — we've got the lot
   The hearts of men to cheer."

And with a flick of practised hands
   Threw open wide his case,
And from the corner of his eye
   Surveyed the old man's face.

THE NEW BREED SALESMAN
Oil on hardboard 45 cm × 35 cm 1976

"There's hair-spray packs for men and boys,
  And fragrant foam shampoo,
Deodorant that stays all day,
  We call it 'Sweetheart True'.

"There's underpants in tangerine,
  In pinks and reds and spots,
And singlets gay, in colours choice,
  Plus multi-coloured lots."

The old man in anger spoke,
  His voice with venom filled,
"Let go the dogs and fetch the whip!"
  The salesman's heart was chilled.

Despite his heavy sample case,
  Unbalanced as he ran,
The new breed salesman cleared the rails
  Just like a deer hound can.

All credit to the bearded one,
  He made it clean away,
And with him all the fancy clothes,
  Deodorant and spray.

No matter where he works today,
  I hope he's making sales
And telling men and boys about
  The day he cleared our rails.

JOHN JAMES MANGAN

A Cuppa' Tea

WHEN you are travelling in the bush or through Australian towns,
When fording flooded rivers, or on drought stricken downs,
Where e'er you go you'll hear these words to welcome you, or me,
"G'day, how are yer goin', mate? Let's have a cuppa' tea."

Though Aussies like their beer, 'tis true, when bent an revelry,
When sweat pours down their torsos they reach for a mug o' tea.
When dust and flies torment their toil, plus aching backs, you'll see
They'll bung the old black billy on, boil up a cuppa' tea.

The whistle blows and workers down their tools for tea respite,
And shearers push their last sheep down the chute with deep delight,
Then rushing from the greasy board shout, "How's the teapot, cook?
Don't tell us you ain't brewed it yet or we'll go mighty crook!"

The ancient swagman ambles on, matilda on his back,
Until he finds a brown lagoon beside the dusty track;
He lights a fire of fallen twigs beneath an old gum tree,
And squats down when his billy boils, to drink a cuppa' tea.

As drovers jog their steady way across the sun-drenched plains,
And heat slows up the cattle — or sheep get bogged by rains —
They spew a string of lurid oaths (unknown by you or me!)
Then grin and drawl, "Aw, what's the odds! Let's brew a cuppa' tea."

The mothers who live in the towns and have to tote a load
Of parcels, babies, up a hill, or down a rutted road,
Dream, as they plod their dreary way, of sitting cosily
With feet up by the kitchen board to have a cuppa' tea.

And when the char drags, weary, home from scrubbing office floors,
The first thing that she does, before she tackles household chores,
Is bang the whistling kettle on, then heaves a sigh, "Oh gee!
Aw gawd! Me achin' feet! I'm dead! Oh, for a cuppa' tea!"

But when the Lady of the House puts on a grand party,
She sets the cakes and savouries out, and serves — genteel coffee!
Then, when the guests have all gone home, she moans, "Oh, deary me!
I really cannot go to bed without my cuppa' tea."

When rugged sportsmen, sports girls too, get scarlet in the face
From prancing round on tennis courts, or running a stiff race,
From playing cricket in the sun, or surfing in the sea,
Or tussling in a football scrum, they swill a cuppa' tea.

And when the people on the course are betting fearful odds
Upon their favourite race horses — which mostly turn out clods —
And they lose all their hard-earned cash upon a "certainty",
"Oh cripes!" they groan, "we're stoney broke! Let's grab a cuppa' tea!"

When children hurt their loving folk with cruel, unthinking words,
The bright plans that they had for life are turned to whey and curds,
And their love's thrown back in their face, be they a he or she,
What do they do? Why, cock a snook! and gulp a cuppa' tea.

When aches and pains tear at their bones, and they are feeling fey,
And friends bring them their tiffs and woes and everything seems grey,
There's only one thing left to do. They cry, "It seems to me
We'd better go and make ourselves a good, strong cuppa' tea!"

When life has caught them by the throat, or shaken them with grief,
And when the one who means the most has proved that love was brief,
When everything they hold most dear does not seem worth the dree,
Then, *"Stone the blanky crows!"* they shout. *"Let's have a cuppa' tea!"*

CLOVER F. NOLAN

A CUPPA' TEA
Oil on hardboard 35 cm × 45 cm 1976

The Mailmen

WELL here's to our mailmen,
All blokes of stirling worth,
Who put up with all kinds of things,
And many an unkind curse.

Their runs are always hard ones,
With no bitumen or such,
But they always seem quite cheerful
And never worry much.

They sometimes have bad weather
To make the going tough,
And if not that then you can bet
That the roads are always rough.

He'll "have a go" at mud and silt
To get the Royal Mail through,
And if he fails you may hear him state,
"Blast that boghole, I've made another blue!"

And when you've finally pulled him out,
And got him on his way,
He goes and breaks an axle
To finalise his day.

They're sometimes nick-named "Four × Four".
You ask why is this so?
Well the reason for this nickname
Is given here below.

Four points of rain in Winton
And they're hardly worth a "zac";
Four *hundred* points won't stop them
When they're finally headed back!!

"SANDY" GLEN HASTED

THE MAILMEN
Oil on hardboard 35 cm × 45 cm 1976

The One Man Town

AT an outback pub in Queensland
as the steam train waited by
filling up with coal and water
(for the track ahead was dry),
we were drinking better liquid,
pots of ice cold Queensland beer
while the publican assured us,
"Southerners are welcome here.
Drink it up and have another,
in the keg there's plenty more."
So we gargled and he told us
how he also owned the store,
ran the bank and was postmaster
of the tiny office there,
took bets of all the shearers,
in his spare time cut their hair.
We'd whiled away a pleasant hour
when a form appeared and roared,
"Finish up! I drive the engine
and it's time you were aboard."
Quite calm the publican advised us,
"Pay no heed, he must be new.
The train won't leave until I say so,
I'm the station master too!"

RUS CENTER

THE ONE MAN TOWN
Oil on hardboard 45 cm × 35 cm 1976

How Banjo Won the Cup

OLD Billy the stockman had gone to his rest
And he gave to me the thing he loved best.
He said, "Take my horse, Banjo's his name.
He may bring you fortune, he may bring you fame."

"He'll go any distance," old Billy had said,
"He hails from the Snowy, he's pure mountain bred.
He's not much to look at, and neither am I,
But he's got a heart as big as the sky."

I met a horse trainer on the race course,
I said, "Will you train him, this game little horse?"
The trainer, a tall bloke, looked up with a frown,
And replied, "If I did I'd be run out of town."

I told him the words that old Billy said,
I told him that Banjo was pure mountain bred,
A mountain or racecourse meant nothing to him,
He'd run till he dropped, with the courage to win.

So Banjo was set for the Sweetwater Cup,
And we took a punt he could win it first up.
The horses he'd meet were the best ever foaled,
The prize was a big one, the cup solid gold.

And though he may look like a goat in disguise,
We all thought that Banjo could take out the prize.
We trained him just right, this game little nag,
And if he came home we'd all win a swag.

Young Ginger the jockey came down from the bush
And he'd hold his own with the smart city push.
He had his instructions, our plans were well laid,
And Ginger on Banjo came out on parade.

The bookies were laughing with tears in their eyes,
"It's any price Banjo!" and to their surprise
We gladly took their five hundred to one.
The crowd yelled, "They're off!" The big race had begun.

Clancy led early, for he had the pace,
And then Pardon's Son, who was well in the race,
And next came Matilda, who had a good show,
And then Jolly Swagman, but where was Banjo?

HOW BANJO WON THE CUP I
Oil on hardboard 35 cm × 45 cm 1976

We picked out his colours out there in the ruck,
He was caught in a pocket, and we cursed our luck;
He was blocked out in front, he blocked from the rear,
And we thought that Banjo would never get clear.

But Ginger the jockey had good riding sense,
He slowly eased Banjo away from the fence,
He found a small gap, was through in a stride,
And the boy from the bush showed them all how to ride.

And people will tell how Banjo got through,
He came down the straight like a bolt from the blue,
He just beat the favourite right there at the post
He won by a whisker from ... Paterson's Ghost!

GEORGE DASEY

HOW BANJO WON THE CUP II
Oil on hardboard 45 cm × 35 cm 1976

Mud Map

HE'D a wall-eyed dog and a bally mare
   And eyes like amber tea,
And he sent the dog to hold the lead
   And drew my road for me.

He smoothed the dust with his brown palm
   As the leaders began to ring,
And cast a prick-eared kelpie bitch
   Out to the spreading wing.

Where roly-polys, mad old hatters,
   Frolic across the sky,
And white as fresh-shorn sheep, the drifts
   Of rustling daisies lie;

By lonely tree, by broken gate
   By creek and star and sun,
There on the plain he carefully showed
   The way my track should run.

A plover scolded the wall-eyed dog,
   The saddles creaked in the heat,
He whistled back the kelpie bitch
   To tongue at his dusty feet.

I shook the drover's knuckley hand
   And thanked him courteously,
But he'll never know how sharp and clear
   He drew my road for me.

ANNE BELL

MUD MAP
Oil on hardboard 35 cm × 45 cm 1976

A Queenslander's Choice

THE Scotsman likes his heather bells,
  The Englishman his rose,
And shamrocks please the Irishman —
  But I choose none of those.

Surrounding my homestead I see,
  And spread far to the west,
The arrows of the sugar cane,
  And these I like the best.

Above maturing sticks of cane,
  In rustling fields of green,
Cane arrows take on many hues
  At different times I've seen.

A QUEENSLANDER'S CHOICE
Oil on hardboard 38 cm × 90 cm 1976

All wet with dew in the sparkling dawn,
  Deep cream when the sun rides high,
Pale mauve when the heavens are overcast,
  Ash-pink from a smoke-filled sky.

But best of all by Queensland eyes,
  I see when day is done,
Erect and tall the arrows stand,
  Silver-lined by the setting sun.

Note: Smoke-filled sky — when cane is being burnt for harvesting.

D.L. MOFFATT

The Railway Hotel

WHEN Joe was a young 'un, his cheeks flecked with down,
He drew his first pay cheque to head into town.
Then up spoke his father: "Son, heed my words well —
Keep clear of the girls at the Railway Hotel.

"Those harpies will fleece you of all that you own,
They're wicked and wanton with hearts as hard as stone.
Believe me, young fella, the road straight to Hell
Begins at the door of the Railway Hotel.

"They'll ply you with whisky, with beer, rum and gin,
Then when you're half sozzled they'll lead you to sin.
They're skilled at seduction, at this they excel —
Those trollops who tempt at the Railway Hotel."

"Gee whiz!" cried our hero, with awe on his face,
"So *that's* what goes on in that old wooden place!
Our parson has warned me of women who dwell
In dens of ill-fame like the Railway Hotel.

"It seems I can still hear that old preacher's words
On drinking and gambling, bad language and birds.
But where did he gain such vast knowledge, pray tell,
Of girls like the ones at the Railway Hotel?"

Joe caught a fast pony and girthed it up tight,
Then, bidding his father a hasty goodnight,
He sprang in the saddle and galloped pell-mell
For his destination — *The Railway Hotel!*

W. G. HOWCROFT

THE RAILWAY HOTEL
Oil on hardboard 45 cm × 35 cm 1976

Where the Bush School Used to Be

THERE'S a dozen different places round the district where you'll see
A pepperina growing and a camphor-laurel tree,
And a pine tree, not a native, and a fence which leans in need
Round a garden bed that struggles 'neath a wilderness of weed;
There's a flagpole still upstanding, but no flag to flutter free,
Not a soul to stand saluting, where the bush school used to be.

Gone the schools, but not forgotten, written in history,
And those bush folk who were pupils have a clinging memory,
Yes, the bush folk, they remember, here their future hopes were born,
Here they heard the lilting bird-song on a spring or summer morn.
And those cold and frosty mornings when their feet were numb and bare,
And their ponies just like dragons puffing steam clouds in the air.

Oh! the news which passed amongst them "standing easy" on the line,
How someone's Dad was cutting chaff and someone's cutting pine,
And the piebald mare at Jones's, she had piebald twins last night,
The Martin kids have measles and the Smith kids have the blight;
And when the flag was hoisted, to attention at command,
Then the teacher spoke with feeling of a noble Motherland.

Oh! the tang of sandwich dinners underneath the "dinner tree",
Where I swapped a "jam" with Mary and she gave a "meat" to me,
Drab those schools I now remember, though in youth we thought them fine,
Each one painted as the other, each one of the same design,
And those teachers, bless the teachers, write their wondrous deeds in stone,
Far from home and friends and family, yet they called these schools their own.

Now the school bus, warm or chilly, and it's never running late,
Does a pick-up in the morning and delivery at the gate —
Yes the whirring and the buzzing on macadam-coated roads,
Of the flashing cars and motor bikes and trucks with heavy loads,
Drown the jingle of the buckles and the creak of saddle straps,
Spoil the scent of sweating ponies and the sheen of saddle flaps.

When you're driving down the highway and you see a vacant spot,
See a flagpole and a pine tree and neglected garden plot,
Hear the glory of the trilling of the early morning song,
See a pony saddled ready where the grass is growing long;
Pause, and listen for a moment by the pepperina tree,
Hear the phantom songs of children, where the bush school used to be.

JOHN JAMES MANGAN

WHERE THE BUSH SCHOOL USED TO BE
Oil on hardboard 35 cm × 45 cm 1976

Rafferty's Ruse

McRankie's camp horse was the best
And swiftest of his breed,
A handsome grey, he broke away
In every test of speed;
But though to see him galloping
Brought us supreme delight,
His owner was unbearable —
The blasted blatherskite!

When picnic races came around,
McRankie made us sore:
He led his horse along the course,
Then showed him off some more;
He scoffed and squinted down his nose
And made unseemly jokes,
Declaring that the rest of us
Rode only nags and mokes.

At length our good friend Rafferty
Evolved a cunning plan;
"I have," said he, "the recipe
To cure this boastful man.
I'll challenge him to have a match,
Myself against the horse,
I'll have him on a hundred yards,
If I can pick the course."

McRankie took the challenge up
And grinned a crooked grin,
"A hundred yards? It's on the cards
I'll have an easy win.
I'll break this fellow Rafferty,
And take him down a peg.
I'll make him eat his words, or else
My head's an addled egg.

"That horse of mine could never lose
On any level track,
On turf or clay he'll show the way,
And I'll be on his back.
We'll spatter mud on Rafferty
Or fill his eyes with dust
And leave him groggy as a man
That's been out on the bust."

RAFFERTY'S RUSE
Oil on hardboard 35 cm × 45 cm 1976

But Rafferty was not deterred
Despite McRankie's threat,
He chose the course to race the horse
And placed a goodly bet.
And did he run and win the match?
That's truly what he did:
The course was fifty yards each side
Of Casey's cattle-grid.

ALF WOOD

Livin' Orf the Land

I FIRST met Jim Blake at Port Douglas,
A haven of sea, sun, and sand.
His method of living intrigued me
In his words 'twas "livin' orf the land".

He was tall, lean and bronzed, and so healthy,
Though three score and ten was his age,
And by our standards he wasn't wealthy,
But from his book, I'd cherish a page.

His possessions were wife, van, and Rover,
Yes ... Margaret was part of his life,
But the Land Rover many times over
Had helped keep them both out of strife.

Jim would drive up the inlet at dawning,
And return with a full bag of crabs,
Then down to the river for prawning,
Catching shellfish for bait, or just yabs.

After lunch he would concentrate spryly,
On catching a number of bream,
Then down to old meat vendor Reilly,
They were caught, he would say, just for him.

He'd mostly land home in the evening
With great lumps of steak in his hands,
Bread, groceries, and things past believing:
This is how old Jim lives orf the land.

Some days he would start up the motor,
And head up the old mountain track,
His shotgun in back of the Rover,
And his rifle strapped on to the back.

His return home would be entertaining,
As he unloaded all of his game,
With continuous bursts of explaining,
Of how he had captured the same.

And as I sit here in the city,
With thoughts of this beautiful land,
I see in my mind's eye, old Jimmy
Just lying flat out on the sand.

His ghost will just haunt me this season,
Lest I go to the boss, out of hand,
Turn my job in, without any reason,
And just try to live orf the land.

ROY E. ANDREWS

LIVIN' ORF THE LAND
Oil on hardboard 35 cm × 45 cm 1976

The Packhorse Drover

Oh the droving life is a life that's free
    On the unfenced routes of the back country,
And a packhorse camp is the place to be
    When they're bringing the store mobs over;
Oh life is happy with not a care
    With the bush smells strong on the balmy air,
For a whiff of the cook would curl your hair
    In the camp of a packhorse drover.

Now the drover's bed is a couch to please
    On the stony ground 'mid the Bogan fleas,
Or in mud that is up to a horse's knees
    When the wintry rains drift over;
But life is happy and life is sweet
    Though there's never enough for a man to eat,
And losing weight is a simple feat
    In the camp of a packhorse drover.

The sky is grey with a hint of rain,
    While the wind blows chill o'er the Rankine plain,
And a ringer swears that he'll drove again
    When the ceiling of Hell frosts over;
But life is happy and life is good
    Round a cow-dung fire when there is no wood,
And the damper tastes as it never should
    In the camp of the packhorse drover.

We watch the mob and we sing the blues,
    And we'd sell our souls for a nip of booze,
As the hours drag by on their leaden shoes
    And the Southern Cross turns over;
It's a rugged life but we never whine,
    For the mateship found in the bush is fine,
Though the boss of course is a hungry swine,
    And a typical packhorse drover.

B. F. SIMPSON

THE PACKHORSE DROVER
Oil on hardboard 35 cm × 45 cm 1976

The Talking Bird

You say you've heard of talking birds? Well, I've known quite a few,
But none as skilled in lingo as O'Reilly's cockatoo.

O'Reilly was an auctioneer whose pride and purse were hurt
When bidding lagged and cleanest goods were sold as cheap as dirt.
He told his wife with emphasis, "It's sad — it's very wrong —
When things are worth a packet and they're knocked down for a song."

O'Reilly thought he'd use a stooge to keep the bidding brisk,
But couldn't find a man who was prepared to take the risk,
Then, just as he decided there was nothing he could do,
Remembered that his uncle had a talking cockatoo.

His uncle was a bullocky, retired some years ago,
Whose speech retained its blueness though his hair had changed to snow;
But while the cocky's language was more rich than other birds',
O'Reilly guessed he had the skill to teach him other words.

When Cocky met O'Reilly's wife, his stocks fell very low;
He called the dame a naughty name and told her where to go.
O'Reilly soon convinced him that was not the way to speak:
He put him in a cage and kept him covered for a week.

Then cunningly O'Reilly worked to prove he was no fool
As day by day he put the cocky through a language school;
At last his care rewarded him with victory, and when
O'Reilly held the hammer up, the bird announced, "Up ten!"

Thereafter when the bidding in the auction room was poor,
The cocky saw the signal from his perch beside the door.
The stratagem worked splendidly, for shrewdly now and then
O'Reilly showed the hammer and the cocky cried, "Up ten!"

Alas! there came disaster, for some thieving joker took
The cocky from the auction room — the low-down, dirty crook!
O'Reilly was disconsolate; he missed the lively bird
And missed the extra dollars when the cocky said the word.

But happiness returned to him before too many days:
O'Reilly saw the bird was back. His heart leaped up with praise.
He saw keen eyes were watching as the bidding lagged; but when
O'Reilly held the hammer up, the cocky cried, "Amen!"

ALF WOOD

THE TALKING BIRD
Oil on hardboard 45 cm × 35 cm 1976

No Less a Son

His name was Sardar Ranjit Singh,
The Mallee was his home,
With filmy silks and spices rich
From town to town he'd roam.

No caste had he: he was a Sikh.
Yet oft' he said to me:
"Before I go, before I die,
I'd leave the wide Mallee.

"Once I lived in Ganga's land,
So very long ago!
And I'd return to that old place —
I hope before I go.

"But should I die before I can
Return to my native shore,
The ashes of this body frail
Shall go to Bangalore."

The years went by and yet it was
But once I met his wife,
And that was after he had gone . . .
After he'd left this life.

She spread his ash on the wide Mallee
And through sobs she made me see:
"He changed his mind towards the end,
His home was the wide Mallee."

CORA PAL

NO LESS A SON
Oil on hardboard 35 cm × 45 cm 1976

A Tale of the Never-Never

ALLOW me to elaborate on a yarn spun by a shearing mate:
It was tucker-time at Newstead and the tea was on the brew,
The subject of his story had long since passed to Glory
But he lived again — as Bill began — in a tale sworn to be true:

"My uncle was a shearer, though some say he was nearer
To a dreamer, judging by the diary that he wrote;
I regard it as his bible, so, safely steering clear of libel,
We'll keep all names fictitious, and, apart from that, I quote:

'In the nineties, I remember, in the bush heat of December,
My mate and I were travelling, in search of work outback;
The end of day was nearing, when in a scrubby clearing
Charley spied a certain something, some ten feet off the track.

'Upon investigation, though it seemed imagination,
The object proved to be a trunk, somewhat small in size:
It was branded *Otis Leather*, it had well kept out the weather
And its contents, speaking mildly, were a very great surprise.

"'Twas the outfit of a minister and, suspecting something sinister,
We searched but could not find the owner, living or deceased;
So, with the best intention, our own welfare not to mention,
We devised a plan to put to use the clothes in the valise.

'Now Charley was a scholar and when he donned the collar
His portrayal of a vicar was artistry to see;
We decided that my part should complement his art
And the role of Charley's "man" it seemed ideally suited me.

'We rode on to a selection, of the squatter asked protection,
The meal his good wife gave us would have satisfied a king;
And I couldn't help but notice as the "Reverend Mr Otis"
Raised his hands in thanks, his finger nails with damper-flour were ringed!

'Next day there was a christening and Charley did the ministering
With a very practised air, it must be told;
Though we refused to take a fee for this service, we agreed
To a "donation" to assist our work in caring for the fold.

'And so we set the pattern (Charley was well-versed in Latin)
For travelling through the country to perform our daily work;
And we married and we christened, and the golden sovereigns glistened
As we gathered in the harvest and our duties never shirked!

A TALE OF THE NEVER-NEVER I
Oil on harboard 35 cm × 45 cm 1976

'And the service we provided for the bush-folk who resided
In the backblocks at that time filled a great and sorry need;
In that cloth-forsaken region, impatient grooms could lose their reason,
Waiting for the travelling clergy, who were very rare indeed!

'After two months of such labour, we thought it in our favour
To desist from further efforts of ministering to the flock;
We shared a growing apprehension of detection (and detention!)
And so it was decided that the "Reverend" be defrocked!

'Charley's outfit was cremated and each of us donated
The sum of twenty sovereigns to the church at Nevertire;
The remainder we'd collected was equally dissected
For we firmly held the labourer was worthy of his hire!

'And if ever you should notice the signature of "Otis"
On a faded, family paper stating marriage vows were sworn,
I would ask you to remember but for our chance find that December
And our dedicated efforts, you might never have been born!'

"Well, that's how Uncle wrote it," said Bill, "just how I have spoke it,
And I never heard him say a word of anything but truth;
And I'd willing make a wager that there's more than one old stager
Who wouldn't be prepared to write so freely of his youth!"

CORAL DASEY

A TALE OF THE NEVER-NEVER II
Oil on hardboard 45 cm × 35 cm 1976

The Gravy Train

I LIVED for many years in the bush — far out — and I starved for lack of rain
Till I slipped the yoke that had kept me broke and caught the Gravy Train;
Now the bridle may rot on the stockyard rail, the shovel in the drain,
And the crowbar rust in the yellow dust, or ever I work again.

The ringers shall strive with the starving stock, but I will not be there —
I'd rather the pub than the gidyea scrub; and I'll weep in my icy beer
When I think of the years I left behind, of the futile fruitless fight
To wrest a home from the stubborn loam, before I saw the light.

We are "the backbone of the land", the politicians say.
There's plenty of sweat and a ton of debt — but bloody little pay;
There's flood and fire and dust and drought, tears and an overdraft,
A wornout wife and a wasted life, rewarding all the graft.

So I've got a job with the Council mob and I live in a house rent free,
And I drive from the bar in a Council car, when I go home to tea.
The cattle may die by the dried-up dam or perish on the plain,
The bank may sweat about the debt — I'm on the Gravy Train.

R. R. DAVIDSON

THE GRAVY TRAIN
Oil on hardboard 35 cm × 45 cm 1976

Storm-Bird

HAVE you heard a storm-bird shrieking in the channels,
When the river bed is cracked and powder-dry,
And the coolibah trees sadly droop, and wither,
As the sheep and cattle round them quietly die?

Have you heard a storm-bird calling from the river,
Its rasping cry, or from the stockyard gate,
And watched the rain clouds roll, and slowly gather,
And prayed they'd burst before it was too late?

Oh, a storm-bird's grating song is stirring music
As it screams, and hurtles by on rapid wings;
For this bird is the bringer of wet seasons,
An omen, to which every bushman clings.

CLOVER F. NOLAN